A SHORT BIOGRAPHY OF JOHN MUIR

A SHORT BIOGRAPHY OF
John Muir

Richard Smith

BENNA BOOKS

Carlisle, Massachusetts

A Short Biography of John Muir

Series Editor: Susan DeLand
Written by: Richard Smith

Copyright © 2018 Applewood Books, Inc.

978-1-944038-54-0

FRONT COVER: *John Muir*, ca. 1917
Orlando Rouland (American, 1871–1945)
Oil on canvas
Gift of Mary W. Harriman, 1920
National Portrait Gallery, Smithsonian Institution

BACK COVER: *John Muir*, ca. 1902
Photograph
Library of Congress

Published by Benna Books
an imprint of Applewood Books, Inc.
Carlisle, Massachusetts

To request a free copy of our current catalog
featuring our best-selling books, write to:
Applewood Books, Inc.
P.O. Box 27
Carlisle, Massachusetts 01741
Or visit us on the web at: www.awb.com

10 9 8 7 6 5 4 3 2 1
MANUFACTURED IN THE UNITED STATES OF AMERICA

JOHN MUIR WAS MANY THINGS: naturalist, writer, inventor, husband, father, environmentalist, philosopher, and glaciologist. Born in Scotland, he made the United States his home, traveling across the country many times as well as around the globe. He saw the divinity of nature and believed it was man's duty to ensure its preservation. Mountains and trees, canyons and glaciers were sacred to John Muir, and he brought to the world's attention the importance of the earth's wild places.

Without him it is likely that there would be no national parks. He was one of the most important and famous naturalists in the world.

John was born in Dunbar, East Lothian, Scotland, on April 21, 1838, the third of eight children to Daniel and Ann Gilrye Muir. His father owned a prosperous grain and feed store and had "an excellent reputation for fair dealing and enterprise." He was also a man with stern religious convictions, and he expected his children to be just as devout. He had been a member of the Church of Scotland but, not finding the church to be strict enough, quit and joined a series of denominations in search of one that fit his religious standards.

Seven of the Muir children were born in Scotland. Only the last sibling, Joanna, would be born in the United States.

Perhaps the strongest childhood influence on John was his grandfather, David Gilrye, who lived nearby. He took the young boy on long nature walks and taught the lad his alphabet and numbers. Young John began his formal schooling at the age of three and, because of his grandfather's tutoring, soon moved up to the second grade. Around the age of seven he advanced to the grammar school in Dunbar, where he learned spelling, math, geography, history, Latin, French, and English. As in many schools of the era, learning was done through rote memorization, and the young students would be beaten with a leather strap for even minor infractions in learning or behavior. John remembered his early schooling as "terrifying," but he loved reading and was particularly attracted to natural history, especially the works of John James Audubon and Alexander Wilson.

"When I was a boy in Scotland I was fond of everything that was wild, and all my life I've been growing fonder and fonder of wild places and wild creatures.

Fortunately, around my native town of Dunbar, by the stormy North Sea, there was no lack of wildness."

Muir would later write that his lessons at school and at home were learned "by heart and by sore flesh."

It was no less strict at home; John's father expected all of his children to memorize the Bible, and any deviation from this learning also led to beatings. As a result, young John had all of the New Testament (and most of the Old) memorized by the age of eleven. His father continued to search for a church that suited his piety and in 1848 joined the religiously conservative Campbellite Church of Christ. In 1849 the family emigrated to the United States. His father planned to move the family to Canada because of a Campbellite community there but soon decided instead to settle in the new state of Wisconsin, where land, farming, and business opportunities were readily available.

The Muirs settled on an isolated eighty-acre farm near the Fox River in Marquette County, Wisconsin. He had explored the hills and dales of Dunbar, and now in America the boy's attraction to the outdoors bloomed. Once the family was settled, John began to explore his new homeland, fascinated with this new world. It was, he later wrote, his "baptism in Nature's warm heart," where "every object excited endless admiration and wonder." Even at eleven years old, nature nourished John Muir's mind, body, and soul.

The life of a farming family was hard on the American frontier. As the oldest boy, John was expected to work the farm alongside his father. Farming was grueling and the workdays were long. The only time John would leave the farm was occasionally to go the ten miles to a nearby town to purchase supplies. Sunday was the sole day of rest. His father's strict hand continued to torment the boy, as did the constant religious instruction; John seemed destined for a life of drudgery and discipline.

Deliverance came from an unlikely source. In 1854 John was hired to help build a road through a nearby bog and met fellow Scotsmen David Gray and David Taylor. The two young men had a love of literature and poetry, and through them Muir rediscovered his own love of the written word. The worlds of Shakespeare, Milton, and others were opened to him, and he voraciously read any and all books he could get his hands on. This obsession with reading continued once he returned to the farm, and he borrowed books from his neighbors when he got the chance.

Muir's father did not approve of nonreligious literature, but John's mother and siblings saw the boy's happiness and helped him hide the offending books. He still worked sixteen-hour days on the farm. He and his father reached a compromise: if John completed his chores and was in

> "Only once was I allowed to leave the harvest field—when I was stricken down with pneumonia."

bed at a reasonable time, he could read in what spare time he had. John began getting up every day at one o'clock in the morning to read before his work began at dawn.

It was evident to all who met him that Muir had a sharp mind and a natural gift for invention. John began tinkering in the basement with his father's tools. Waterwheels, windmills, clocks, an "early rising machine" (an ingenious device that tipped him out of bed before dawn), and a "field thermometer" all sprang from Muir's imagination and were built with wood scraps. In September 1860 he was encouraged by a neighbor to exhibit some of his inventions at the state agricultural fair in Madison, Wisconsin. Although his father was against the idea, Muir, now almost twenty-two years old, decided to take his inventions to the fair; it was a decision that would change his life.

His inventions were a huge success in Madison. He received a $15 honorarium

Young Muir was particularly attracted to the poetry of a fellow Scotsman, Robert Burns. He would often take a volume of Burns with him on his walks.

for his work and was even declared "a genius" by the exhibit judges. Most importantly, he made connections. One of the judges was Jeanne Smith Carr, the wife of a science teacher at the University of Wisconsin, and she and Muir became friends. Muir used this friendship to enroll at the university in the spring of 1861. He paid his own way, lived in a boardinghouse, and worked at odd jobs. He kept a spartan diet to save money, surviving on mush made from whole wheat flour and an occasional potato.

Jeanne Carr was an influence on Muir. Starting in 1866, they enjoyed a lifelong correspondence about life and nature.

Although the lack of money ended Muir's college life after two and one-half years, he made the most of it, taking a wide variety of classes including chemistry, math, physics, Greek, Latin, botany, and geology. This wasn't a regular course of study, but Muir took classes based on his interests and not on the idea of earning any sort of degree. By 1863 he decided that it was time to take an extended trip through the northern states into Canada. He was, he later wrote, going "away on a glorious botanical and geological excursion" into the "University of the Wilderness."

"I was tormented with soul hunger. I was on the world. But was I in it?"

Thus began Muir's lifelong penchant for travel. He became a self-proclaimed "tramp." The Civil War was raging into its third year and Muir, morally opposed to war, wanted nothing to do with it. He took a summer trip down the Wisconsin River, across the Mississippi River, and over the Iowa bluffs. His Canada excursion included Lake Huron, Georgian Bay, and Niagara Falls. He stopped in Meaford, Canada, and lived with his brother Dan (who was avoiding the war) for the next two years, working in a broom factory. John spent his free time collecting plant specimens and botanizing.

It is a myth that Muir was a draft dodger. In fact, his name was never called for service in the Union army.

Near the end of 1866, Muir returned to the United States and settled in Indianapolis, working at a factory that manufactured wagon parts. It was here that another life-changing event occurred when, working late at night, a file he was using slipped from his hand and pierced his right eye, blinding him. He also lost the sight in his left eye. Muir spent several months in a darkened room, fearing that he would be blind for the rest of his life. His eyesight slowly returned, but the accident led Muir to seriously reconsider his life and his priorities. He made a vow that, if his sight were to return, he would travel the world to explore and experience the wonders of nature.

The immune response known as "sympathetic blindness" caused his left eye to lose sight. This assisted in healing, and soon sight was restored to both eyes.

With this new mind-set, Muir decided to take a trip "sufficient to...brighten my after life in the gloom and hunger of civilization's defrauding duties." He took the train from Indianapolis to Louisville, Kentucky, and from there walked to the Gulf of Mexico, a journey of over a thousand miles. With a New Testament, John Milton's *Paradise Lost,* and the poems of Robert Burns, he tramped through Kentucky and into Tennessee and Georgia, keeping notes on the natural phenomena and commenting on the effects of the recently ended Civil War on the landscape. From Savannah, he walked across Florida to Cedar Key and its tiny adjacent islands in the Gulf of Mexico. The trip took almost three months to accomplish. Muir's grand excursion would be published posthumously in 1916 as *A Thousand-Mile Walk to the Gulf.*

Muir's plan had been to go on to South America, but a bout with malaria ended this journey.

After recuperating from malaria, Muir continued his wandering ways. He spent a month in Cuba, then went north to New York City, but, not surprisingly, he hated the crowds and size of the city. He then decided to go to California by steamer via the Isthmus of Panama. Muir landed in San Francisco and headed east on foot to the Sierra Nevada. Here he was awestruck by the majesty of the peaks and waterfalls. In 1869 he took a job herding 2,000 sheep to Tuolumne Meadows in the High Sierra. He documented this experience in his book *My First Summer in the Sierra*. Muir found his life's purpose in the Sierra; it was love at first sight. He climbed the staggering peaks with sheer faces, studying their nature and recording his thoughts. He wrote about the mountains and valleys of Yosemite for national publications. He constructed a cabin with a creek running beneath it and live ferns growing through the floorboards—he slept hearing the water and breathing the mountain plants.

John Muir and Yosemite would become inseparable, forever connected in our national memory.

The early 1870s saw Muir involved with the study of glaciers and their effect on the creation of the Sierra Nevada. He became involved in controversy and was ridiculed when he disagreed with leading geologists over the origins of the mountains; while Muir believed (correctly) that glaciers were responsible for the California landscape, others believed that the mountains and valleys were randomly created by catastrophic geologic forces. In December 1871 Muir published his first essay, "Yosemite Glaciers," in the *New York Tribune*, and his well-articulated theories of glaciation won him many followers. Ralph Waldo Emerson, elderly then, visited Mariposa Grove and spoke at length with Muir about geology and plant life in the area. Over the next few years Muir began a yearly routine of exploring the Sierra Nevada during the summer and living in Oakland during the winter, writing up his explorations for various periodicals. In particular, he found a home for his articles with the *Overland Monthly*, a California literary magazine.

In 1872 and 1873 Muir would publish six essays about various aspects of Yosemite in the magazine.

But Muir was lonely. "In all God's mountain mansions I find no human sympathy, and I hunger," he wrote a friend. In 1874, he met twenty-seven-year-old Louisa (Louie) Wanda Strentzel, the daughter of a prosperous fruit farmer in Martinez, California. As Muir's fame grew, he continued to write and lecture (despite stage fright), and all the while he and Louie grew closer. She shared his love of botany and didn't seem to mind his extended excursions into the mountains. In June of 1879, just before Muir took his first voyage to Alaska, he and Louie agreed to be married on his return. He would be gone for six months.

John and Louie were married on April 14, 1880. They had two children; Wanda was born in 1881 and Helen in 1886. In 1890, the family moved into a home given to them by Louie's parents, a seventeen-room Victorian mansion. Muir took over the 2,600-acre Strentzel fruit farm and fell into the comfortable life of a family man. His wife and friends eventually urged him to start writing again. He retired from active ranching and returned to writing.

The farm brought in a sizable income by growing a wide variety of fruit and nuts.

Muir began working on a collection of California nature studies, *Picturesque California*.

John Muir's domesticity did not stop him from his wanderings, with two excursions to Alaska between 1880 and 1890. In 1889 he began the work he would be best remembered for, the campaign to have Yosemite preserved for future generations. He saw Yosemite and the Sierra Nevada as a pristine land and he wanted it to stay that way. The area had been overrun by sheep farmers, and Muir saw them as the biggest threat to Yosemite's existence. In 1889, Muir befriended Robert Underwood Johnson, an influential editor for *Century Magazine*. Johnson visited Yosemite with Muir and saw the damage a large flock of sheep had done to the area. He agreed to publish any articles Muir wrote on the subject of excluding livestock from the Sierra. He would also use his influence to introduce a bill in Congress to make the

In his writings, Muir called sheep "hoofed locusts."

Yosemite area into a national park. Thanks mainly to John Muir's efforts, the Yosemite National Park would be created in 1890.

Muir's writing fed his reputation as a conservationist. He was now known outside of California, and his fame spread throughout the country. He wrote articles for various magazines and was interviewed by newspapers, which helped spread his gospel of conservation. He became a champion for the preservation of natural wonders outside of California, such as the Grand Canyon and the Petrified Forest in Arizona, and was influential in the preservation of these places. He encouraged city dwellers to get out into the wilderness and experience the wonders of nature firsthand. In particular, he insisted that people should visit the country's national parks to reinvigorate their spirit. The parks were, he wrote, "places for rest, inspiration, and prayers."

It was because of Muir's growing fame

Muir wrote of the Grand Canyon: "It seems a gigantic statement for even nature to make.... Wildness so godful, cosmic, primeval."

that he was approached by Joachim Henry Senger, a professor at the University of California, with the idea of forming an association for mountain lovers. Around this same time, Muir's *Century Magazine* editor, Robert Underwood Johnson, who'd worked with Muir on the campaign to create Yosemite National Park, also made a similar suggestion. Muir liked the idea. In May 1892 he met with a small group of devotees in San Francisco, and the Sierra Club was born. This new organization was modeled after the Appalachian Mountain Club, organized in Boston in 1876. Naturally, Muir was chosen to be the Sierra Club's first president. The club's early goals included successfully establishing the Glacier and Mount Rainier National Parks and, after Muir's death, went on to support creation of the National Park Service in 1916.

In 1894 Muir had his first book published by the Century Company, *The*

Muir would hold the position of the Sierra Club's first president until his death in 1914.

Mountains of California. The book was well received and with literary fame came more travel. Muir was now a man of the world. He went to New York, where he met the likes of Mark Twain, Rudyard Kipling, Nikola Tesla, and the naturalist John Burroughs. A quick trip to Boston found him in Concord, Massachusetts, where he laid flowers on the graves of his literary heroes, Ralph Waldo Emerson and Henry David Thoreau. While in Massachusetts he also met the writer Sarah Orne Jewett and the historian Francis Parkman. World travel soon followed, with Norway, Switzerland, Italy, and the United Kingdom on his itinerary. Muir made his first return to Dunbar, Scotland, and later in the year began a yearly tradition of sending money to his cousins for distribution to the poor of Dunbar.

Muir became a tireless worker for governmental protection of wilderness areas. He constantly lobbied politicians

While in Concord, Muir visited Walden Pond, where Thoreau lived in a small, one-room house from 1845 to 1847.

to support land conservation, and he personally wrote hundreds of letters to congressmen, senators, and even presidents to gain support for preserving the nation's forests. In 1898 he wrote an article for the *Atlantic Monthly* entitled "Wild Parks and Forest Reservations of the West," an essay that ignited the public's support for the preservation of America's wild places. Muir's adopted countrymen were beginning to take his words to heart.

> *"Thousands of tired, nerve-shaken, over-civilized people are beginning to find out that going to the mountains is going home; that wildness is a necessity."*

Institutions of higher learning now began to recognize the importance of Muir and his work. Harvard University conferred the honorary degree of master of arts on him in 1896; the University of

Wisconsin followed in 1897 with a doctor of laws (LL.D.); and the same degree was conferred on him by the University of California in 1913. In 1911 Muir also received the degree of doctor of literature from Yale.

The twentieth century dawned, and John Muir, now a man in his sixties, seemed as tireless as ever. He continued his political work but never lost his love of wandering in the woods. Always the dedicated family man, it was evident to his wife that "his heart remained wild." If John seemed restless or cranky, Louie would "shoo him back up" to his mountains. He might be gone for hours or even days. Sometimes he would take his daughters with him, and he always returned home reinvigorated, his health and spirits restored.

On his walks Muir usually carried a sack filled with only bread and tea, saying that was all he needed for surviving in the wilderness.

In May of 1903 Muir made one of the most important connections of his life when he was asked by President Theodore Roosevelt to guide him through the Sierra and Yosemite. The two men had corresponded but had never met, and, knowing that he was going to be visiting Yosemite, Roosevelt knew that Muir was the only one who could show him around: "Of course of all the people in the world, he was the one with whom it was best worth while thus to see the Yosemite," Roosevelt would write. "I do not want anyone with me but you, and I want to drop politics absolutely for four days and just be out in the open with you."

Roosevelt was followed by a huge contingent of staff, dignitaries, and newspaper reporters. He and Muir managed to give them the slip and, with two pack mules bearing their camping supplies, they went deep into the woods and camped among the giant sequoias. Their trip started at the Mariposa Grove and included Sentinel Dome, Glacier Point, Yosemite Valley, and other points of interest in the park. Roosevelt wrote, "There can be nothing in the world more

Roosevelt and Muir spent three days together in Yosemite.

beautiful than the Yosemite, the groves of the giant sequoias and redwoods, the Canyon of the Colorado, the Canyon of the Yellowstone, the Three Tetons; and our people should see to it that they are preserved for their children and their children's children forever, with their majestic beauty unmarred." They spent the entire trip talking about nature and conservation. Roosevelt, a lifelong birder, was a little surprised when Muir didn't know the various birdsongs they heard. Muir, for his part, did his best to dissuade the president from his "childish" practice of hunting. Even so, the two men enjoyed their time together, and the trip accomplished what Muir hoped it would: Roosevelt became the first president to take an active role in land preservation. Three years later Roosevelt signed the Antiquities Act, a precursor to the National Park Service which obligated federal agencies to preserve "scientifically,

Many of the sequoia trees are over 1,000 years old.

culturally and historically valuable sites." Roosevelt would sign into existence 5 national parks, 18 national monuments, 55 national bird sanctuaries and wildlife refuges, and 150 national forests.

In the summer of 1903 Muir embarked on an extended world tour, encompassing Europe and Asia. His companions on the first leg of the journey were botanist and Harvard University professor Charles Sprague Sargent and his son. They traveled through London, Paris, and Berlin, visiting museums and art galleries—so many that Muir declared he had seen "enough for a life-time."

From there it was on to Finland and Russia. Instead of museums, galleries, and palaces, Muir explored the outdoors and visited the Caucasus Mountains and the Black Sea. They took the train across Siberia, through the wheat fields and forests of the Volga to Vladivostok. From there they continued on to Shanghai, China.

In his lifetime Muir visited six continents, over a dozen states and territories, and more than seventeen countries.

Here, Muir and the Sargents parted ways, with Muir going on to explore India to see the deodar forests and the lofty Himalaya Mountains. On his way back to America he visited Australia, the Mueller Glacier in New Zealand, and Hong Kong and China; explored the forests of the Philippines; gazed at Fujiyama dimly through the haze from the deck of the ship; and saw Hawaii. Muir, then sixty-six-years old, arrived home after traveling for almost a year.

In May 1905 Louie Muir became seriously ill, diagnosed with a lung tumor. She died at the Muir home on August 6, 1905. John was grief-stricken, devastated by his wife's death. Through twenty-five years of marriage she had been his staunch supporter, unselfishly encouraging him to write and even sending him to the mountains when he was becoming too civilized. She knew that he needed to go on his excursions, to follow his heart. In 1888 she wrote a letter to him, explaining why

Louie Strentzel Muir was fifty-eight years old when she died.

he needed to continue his wanderings: "A ranch that needs...the sacrifice of a noble life...ought to be flung away beyond all reach....The Alaska book and the Yosemite book, dear John, must be written, and you need to be your own self."

Over the next few years Muir wrote and published his most popular books: *Stickeen: The Story of a Dog* (1909); *My First Summer in the Sierra* (1911); and *The Story of My Boyhood and Youth* (1913). All were well received and popular. Ironically, Muir did not like writing. He found it tedious and was often unhappy with the results. Had it not been for the continued encouragement from his wife and editors it is likely that Muir would not have left behind the body of work that he did. In his lifetime Muir published over 300 articles and 12 books.

"One day's exposure to mountains is better than a cartload of books."

In 1911 the seventy-three-year-old Muir took his last excursion and fulfilled a lifelong ambition to explore the Amazon River. His daughters and friends tried to stop him from going, but he would not be deterred. He sailed up the Amazon, then down the coast of South America to Buenos Aires. He then took a train across the continent to Chile to see the Aurucaria forests, then, returning to Argentina, he boarded a ship for Africa, intent on seeing a baobab tree. He found the tree near Victoria Falls at the Zambia-Zimbabwe border. Returning home to California in April of 1912, he had been gone for almost eight months.

"One of the greatest of the great tree days of my lucky life."

Starting in 1907, Muir became involved in one last battle for land preservation when the City of San Francisco wanted to dam up the Tuolumne River in the Hetch Hetchy Valley to create a water reservoir for the city. The Hetch Hetchy lies within the boundary of Yosemite National Park, and naturally Muir opposed the dam. The battle went on for years, and upon his return from Africa in 1912 he renewed his campaign to save Hetch Hetchy. But Muir's fight was in vain; in 1913 Congress passed, and President Woodrow Wilson signed, the Raker Act, which permitted the flooding of the valley and the creation of the O'Shaughnessy Dam. It would be the last preservation battle of John Muir's life.

Muir would write to a friend about the dam, "It is a monumental mistake, but it is more, it is a monumental crime."

John Muir was in failing health for the last two years of his life. He attempted to finish the book he was writing about his excursions to Alaska, but in December 1914, while visiting his daughter Helen in Daggett, California, Muir developed pneumonia. His doctors saw the seriousness of his illness, and he was soon admitted to the California Hospital in Los Angeles. He died on December 24, 1914. The world mourned, with the *Los Angeles Times* reporting, "America has lost perhaps its greatest naturalist, the world one of its most remarkable nature poets." John Muir was seventy-six years old. He was buried in the family plot on the Martinez ranch, next to his beloved Louie.